It will happen by chance
and other poems

MOSAÏQUEPRESS

First published in 2024

MOSAÏQUE PRESS
Registered office:
Bank Gallery
High Street
Kenilworth, Warwickshire
CV8 1LY

Compiled by Christopher M James

ISBN 978-1-906852-23-8

Preface

This collection contains work by members of the French Online Poetry Stanza group, an affiliate of The Poetry Society. A majority of the poems have been shared and critiqued during Stanza sessions and have been chosen to highlight the considerable diversity of talent that a Stanza group can and should nurture and stimulate. Many of these poems have been published in the UK, USA, Canada or Ireland, as referenced in the Acknowledgements on page 64.

For poets writing in English who may feel isolated in their respective regions across France and who are willing to discover and share work, this group offers a supportive and vibrant environment. Twice-monthly online meetings available for some fifty members have fostered an enthusiastic, inclusive and dynamic group. New members are always welcome: please contact Christopher M James at *ohmercy5@yahoo.fr*

Contents

Sharon Black

Café des Arts

What could be better at ten a.m.
than espresso, croissant and freshly pressed
orange juice at a table on rue St. Guilhem?

Somewhere else, big wheels are turning;
a factory worker is being fired,
an oil rig's sprung a leak,

a head of corporation is dabbing his wife's cheek
as she weathers a contraction:
eight billion lives revolving on their axles.

Here on St. Guilhem, an electric UPS van
glides between lit facades,
between a toddler in a pushchair

and a woman in red jeans with a matching caddy,
between two ladies with four dogs on leads
and a cyclist.

It meets a white van, reverses, pulls in to the side,
lets the petrol engine blather past.
Eight billion revolutions

in the time it takes to drink a coffee,
drain an orange juice, dab up buttery flakes,
the biggest then the smallest.

Sharon Black

Folio

after a photograph by Álvaro Alejandro

Hard to tell if these are my words
on wood pulp pressed to paper
or the tree's own testimony.

Take this fallen leaf. Our veins are
indistinguishable. They snake and crisscross
under near-transparent panels.

The story is one I haven't read,
in a language I never learned. It doesn't
falter at the spine but rises

through the skin into
a library of trees, I don't know what species.
Look how each peels back its bark,

its quiet sapwood, until what is left
is light. It wants to show
how we are so alike.

Its limbs – arched to shelter me from rain –
are breakable. And my veins
are blue-green, like an egg.

There's always so much more to say.
The secret is to push your thoughts
into the ground. Observe. Then

write down what you see.
This is what the canopy strives for day after day,
what it will always deliver.

Nina Bogin

The Swifts

You who loved the swifts,
did you know the day would come
when the swifts would abandon you?

When the evening sky, crossed
by their paths, would ignore you,
the world pursue its course

without a backward glance?
I sit on the steps leading
down to the garden

and take in what leaves you out,
the grass, the roses, the pink and red
impatiens in their earthenware pots,

children's exuberant shouts
from the park across the river,
the swifts' last cries before night.

We knew the swifts come only in summer,
knew summer lasts only so long,
we couldn't know

how deep the silence is
when we ourselves have flown.

Nina Bogin

Wooden Spoons

If spoons have souls it's because
our hands have burnished them
with the warmth of our grip

mingling with the seasons
embedded in their grain.
Upright in a pitcher

like a stand of trees in winter,
they still weather the passage of time.
Take this spoon, its handle warped,

the chipped edge of its scoop
in a lopsided smile – it's the one
I reach for when I stir the soup, that's

curved to my palm, my gestures.
Does the spoon know me as I know it?
Sometimes it knows me too well.

I picture you in the kitchen
peeling apples and quinces,
cooking compote in a saucepan –

as if tasks outlived us.
As if I took the stirring spoon
from your hand.

Tango

Waiting for the porridge pot to boil
I practice Argentine tango
Extending first one leg, then the second;
And the silver kettle's gravid belly
Mirrors me in my blue nightgown:
My spine is straight, my arms curve round
As if around a beach ball,
Or that red balloon the sun
Just rising from the puzzled rooftops.
One street over I see a girl
Jump to catch a string she never
Thought could slip away so fast. . .

> *Mind what you're doing, or you'll fall!*
> *Move your right foot forward,*
> *Brush your left instep; flex*
> *Your knees the way Natasha said. . .*

Natasha Ng from Buenos Aires,
Who won't allow us to Embrace
Or dance *Cruzada* and *Boleo*
Until we learn to walk. *Caminar.*
Sun floods the room in the kettle:
Slotted spoon, plate of fruit, the copper scales
To weigh and measure
From my husband's mother's Marseille pharmacy;
We could be a portrait, I think,
A picture of a Woman in a Kettle.

Beverley Bie Brahic

The Origin of Art

Near Corinth, Pliny has it, lived a girl
whose love promised to be true
as he sailed off on business for a while,

winds uncertain. She lit a lamp
and cast his shadow on the wall,
next she drew a line around him.

Her dad, a potter, made a model
of the profile he fired with his pots –
Now, you can hold love's silhouette.

So sculpture started, Pliny says,
to let us hold the pictures
we project upon our walls. Pliny says

a line marks the end of something,
a horizon, border or extremity
that keeps the figure from the background,
            our losses in the offing.

Nejra Ćehić

I read some poets

and it's like the day we leave
El Calafate — stand
    before the great
        glacier, crumbling chunks big as
houses, a solid fact, from a distance
    felt in our bodies like an earthquake
        in a faraway country

We hear the glacier's seasonal
        meltdown / gunfire / gamelan
            dissonance
    with the sight of falling ice, lightning coming
  after thunder.   Our mouths
un-shut — thirst for
    beauty & devastation all at once.
The guide tells us the glacier is in
    stasis, not the reason for rising
sea levels. This is not a dying
    being, why are we crying?

Summer in the southern hemisphere
blooming
      the berry that gave
        this town its name. Blue & pink
ice melts, purple fruit stains
    our lips, the tips of our fingers
in El Calafate — we touch
that day
      breaking

Nejra Ćehić

a request

If this body   dies   before   you

       wash me   in fire

                  mix my ashes

       with earth ochre

                &   water

to soak a silk cloth

       wear it wherever

                  you want

to be kissed

Jennefer Cole

The Art of Nest Building

Out the kitchen window stands
the skeleton of a tree, just before

the tender green shoots shoot through
to live on a sapling's scaffolding.

Two magpies fly about, inspect old nests
hanging empty, pull a twig, place it here,

move it there, force a fit, in a fit of force.
They look bird-brained – slender sticks

in beaks, rushing around – but must know
the art of what they do. Funny, I am so blind

to see. Pencil in hand, I push and pull
to fit the words in lines just so,

like magpie gatherings, collections
of shiny moments I steal to write.

Nightly Negotiations

Two women rise between 3 and 5.
One drinks some milk, turning her
naked front from the fridge's glare,
always hopeful this will do the trick.

The other goes to check their breathing,
pull up blankets, push down bent knees,
monitor life. One regrets not taking that
pill and shakes her head at the absurdity.

The other sits to write the unsaid words
in her head, folded over sheets of paper,
arms tight to protect from cold air.
One looks at the anonymous darkness.

She traces the moon's path, & curls up inside
me, oblivious to the possible *schadenfreude*.
The other knows how a star becomes a void,
how with time, small things become large.

David Crann

The summer the child died

I am marked this summer
by passing shadows
of the passing of the child who drowned
asking nothing of me but
the taut calamity of tears.

Were I tattooed with eagles
I would soar. Tattooed
with inken images I sink
and leave indelible traces of me
in his story
which I do not merit
and he does not deserve.

Wracked with floral tributes,
his small bed in the graveyard
lures me back.

I cannot bear him
cold and lonely slowly
surrendering beneath.

I read him stories
he cannot read
and sing him songs
he cannot hear.

He wipes my eyes with fingers
he will never touch his mother with.

His bed creaks in the night
and a listening owl
bows in silent homage,
the odd but only nursemaid.

David Crann

When I am an old man

When I am an old man
and become a child, I shall think as a child –
as far as thinking remains an option.

I shall hold the paper with which I wipe my arse
in the other hand
and masturbate from memory, shunning glossy magazines.

I shall hold my erection over the district nurse
like a votive offering
and come in intermittent bursts
subject as ever to a depression over the Azores.

I shall piss with studied imprecision
(a hosepipe pinched at random intervals)
and shit only on odd-numbered days
and on alternate sides of the road,
avoiding parking fines and letting my mind
squat on traffic wardens and politicians.

I shall wear women's underwear,
not out of perverseness, but in the hope
a road accident will make me interesting
to family and friends.

I shall hum at funerals,
and wink at weddings at the bridesmaids
to encourage libels
(reaching for my lawyer).

I shall suck my soup from distance
because I can,
and would grind my teeth to irritate –
but cannot – damn it!

I shall mention conkers, non-electric typewriters,
steam engines, shunting, and multiple orgasm
to whet the inquisitiveness of great-grandchildren;
and mention sodomy and monastic condominiums
to rekindle priests.

When I am an old man
I shall kick dead leaves,
the cat (when no one's looking)
and ass;

and I shall talk to all the dead people I know
and who are with me so much more
than those who are here alive,
the same those whom I love, when I remember,
and who – when I remember – make me weep.

I shall glide into sleep
regretting nothing – with a passion –
excepting sleep.

And I shall die at the most inconvenient moment
out of sheer bloody-mindedness
in a rare lucid interval.

Anne Eyries

The End of Endurance, 1915

From your crow's nest no opening in sight
to allay your restless oscillations;
men, dogs, one cat, trapped in unrelieved white,
crushed by floes and hopeless expectations.
You drift for months through half grey frozen light
wintering this wilderness, crew weary
of fearful creaks and groans that plague each night.
Your seams crack at last, screaming an eerie
obbligato. Masts crash, dogs howl with fright
and pumps churn in your bowels for no reward.
Shackleton orders all out on the ice:
Hurley cranks me up again to record
your final throes. My epic film, sealed tight
in double tins, will one day be restored.

Gill Foster

Love story

They staggered on as slow
As they dared across the snow,
Feet freezing and bleeding, lips starved and cracked.
His arm was about her waist, hers about his neck.
She whispered, *If you love me, let me go.*
He said, *Never my love, I'll not let you go.*
But again she said, *If you love me, let me go.*
He bent his head, she raised her mouth to his,
One last kiss then he let her drop upon the snow.
He did not look back when he heard the crack
Of the bullet ending her pain
But trudged on across the snow.
He thought his heart would burst
As her words echoed in his brain,
If you love me, let me go.

Another time, another place,
And, close to his, another face.
Cocooned warmly in sheets white as snow,
He raised a hand to caress her smooth cheek,
He whispered, *If you love me, let me go.*
She said, *Never my love, I'll not let you go.*
But again he said, *If you love me, let me go.*
A brief nod, a tearful smile and a last kiss.
He knew then she'd tell the white coats, *Enough. No more.*
He heard her high heels clacking on the tiled floor
He knew that she would not look back
His thin hand smoothed the white sheet.
He thought his heart would burst
Knowing he had been twice blessed,
Murmured, *I loved them both, I let them go.*

Mary Gilonne

Papermaker

Water-logged with aspen, larch and fir, he takes cream pulp,
settles it down sweet as curds, paddles a long dark
oar across and rests. A quiet surface of page shores up
along the frame and ferries his thoughts to monasteries,
a meditative marsh of birds, her wading thighs like gleaming carp.
He can almost hear a fishering of bells drifting lines across the Broads
see Ludham floating, hardly moored to any land-locked thing.
Rimed, his hands hang parchment white, salted,
drying this absence of her. She has nearly gone,
only a shoal of books and bags, bones of little things are left,
her waiting shoes bask delicate as minnows. He's watermarked,
hold him to light, see how the press of her is printed through him.

Mary Gilonne

It will happen by chance

'Don't think the garden loses its ecstasy in winter, it's quiet but the roots are down there riotous.' – Rumi

that elusive epiphany. A stranger's palms,
      conched around cup or book
one café morning, will recall to me others
      with their sudden curved rapture.

It'll happen when I'm autumning through scuffs of yellow
      leaves, scrag end of days
and plate-glass skies leaning heavy. A swifting bright
      will pick out among Holt's trees,

wish-bones of old places where I loved
      the first or last with him and him and him.
It'll startle in a pub's dark corner
      flaring with disremembered laughter,

or by that pegged jacket its wooling still warm with lost arms.
      Some days wild hazel hedges will shoulder me close
like longing suitors down lust-forgotten lanes
      and a flushed treacle-taste of skin

will surprise my tongue once more.
      It will happen when tumbled fruit-fall drifts
with humming heat, sedgy midge-shade pools
      full of voices surfacing, lapsed desires

treading water, and I'll gasp this in-between.
      All is in light's wing, I'm neither here nor there,
time and people dovetail fitfully.
      It'll happen, happen by chance.

Kathleen Gray

Déjà Vu

It isn't big events she remembers most,
though there's nothing wrong

with her memory, or her eyes, following
every movement he makes

in her stuffy hospice room. He opens windows
wide, letting in the half-forgotten growl of traffic

on the boulevard below. He stands a moment,
arms outstretched the way hers used to spread

as he ran to her across the schoolyard clamour
the winter his father left.

Nicholas Henshall

I never got to Mt Fuji

Going out in the late afternoon into the country by train from Tokyo
Green hills, black cemeteries, all full
Come alive in my eye

Houses bunch together
People hover at crossroads
Phone cables lace the horizon
Trees seem eerie, somehow silent

Boys in my compartment hide behind manga books
Busy themselves with each other and the way they look
Further down, salarymen get raucous and fat on Kirin beer

Japan is the colour of black slate
Bricks black, wooden houses black
An orange sun lowers a little –
The prospect of Mount Fuji is gripping

A winding road runs parallel to the railway track
I see a bridge straddling the valley far away fading
We leave the sun behind, twisting and turning in its shadow

One of the men pulls a window curtain to one side
Puffs eagerly on his cigarette, sips beer
He seems not to see the land, the trees, the streams
As we slide through the hills on to Odawara
And our destination: Hakone Yumoto

I am here alone
Dusk is falling, train racing
Once it stops, getting to Mount Fuji will take another hour by bus

Kate Hill-Charalambides

Burnt Milk

As she stood at our doorway
my body took her in with closed lips.
She poured it all out.

I couldn't make the frothing milk recede into the pan.
I couldn't calm the blubbering,
steady the hand;
or roll the tears back up her face into the ducts.
Nor siphon it all into the bottle for the icebox.

Begin before his name scorched in her mouth.
Before she ran through the streets naked.
Before the probative officer forced her into a van.
Before the day
they took her baby away.

Jill Husser

Birthing

We didn't expect you so soon
        but waves broke on the beach
drew back with strength

        over soft stones
and I was tossing flotsam.
        The girl with the ponytail

in a blue overall
        was minding the monitors
as grey seals chased

        wild salmon in the Sound.
And then you were there,
        in the glare

of the hospital prefab,
        washed up and waxy
on the shore:

        your tiny form enfolded
in a sheep shawl
        with yellow flags, sea pinks.

Christopher M James

Marshes

Wind combs the cordgrass
parting the hair on a lost sea's scalp.
Drops of rain punctuate

the half-light with air quotes.
From this distance, we listen for
the cries of snipes feeling their way,

foraging mud's tunnels.
A peewit's call of distress
is emptied of all irony.

A sole heron dares a neck.
Far down the path
a birdwatcher sifts the evidence;

his hands rise, drop, rise
as if rubbing his eyes, unsure.
He leans forward, peering

through a keyhole into sky.
An artist, with a court
of canvasses and paints,

pares down the patterns of light,
probing the riddle
of what won't answer back.

Must he add the birds from memory?
Is he searching for
nature's vanishing point?

Our side, we think
we're close to a stash of plovers,
but their world too

is thin-skinned now:
we crouch, our over-whispering
released like a bowling ball,

sends one wader alone,
snappish into air
and away.

Christopher M James

Traces

Isaan, the vast rice-growing plateau
in north-east Thailand

Endless paddies
stencil the land, enmesh the living.
Their waters smudge

a setting sun's inks. A hand
has wiped leftover pigments
on a cloth of sky.

A motorcycle
scratches the land
for epidermic dust, guessing

a low track, up to
a corrugated iron scar
of an outbuilding. What

pinprick of space is yours here?
The same as an old lady's,
squatting at a roadside. Your

boyhood world globe was a skin
encircling a lamp, which you spun
for all your tales to come. Now

you recall the rare times when,
dauntless, half-aware,
you tattooed the ready earth.

Shirin Jindani

#MakingFriends

I had no friends and so I made them out of odds and ends —
a torn sheet, last year's fraying shirt, two mismatched gloves
— were stuffed with plastic wrappers, bits of string, the viscera
of unpaid bills; all bound by an invisible seam.
I sewed their torsos to some cut-off jeans.

Feet were easy, heads were not, asymmetric faces watched
as buckled shoes hung on pendulum legs. Inarticulate,
inclined to rip, they held their counsel zipper-lipped
and when a button-eye rolled across the floor,
the remaining eye stared even more.

They were happy, at least I think they were, my patchwork tribe
about chest height. They had woollen hair (some were bald)
and broadly respected social norms. They sat at tables,
lounged on chairs, wore reading glasses to check their phones
and posted selfies when left alone.

Evenings we basked in the aquarium light of deep-sea documentaries
unaware that my cloth companions had sparked a global trend.
The viral storm broke after a series of revenge porn pics
exposed the *Extravagant genitalia* of my *Hand-sewn Freaks*.
In a non-binary world, I believe we are all biologically unique.

After a papier-mâché shark surfaced in the bed
I furloughed my friends. Now a hermit crab occupies the reading lamp.
Decked out in snorkel and diving mask, I meet the raised eyebrows
of the supermarket manager scanning fruit
as he weighs up my home-crocheted-Lurex-all-in-one wetsuit.

31

Charlie Lomas

Aunt Elizabeth's Cousin Ethel

On my first Edinburgh trip,
cousin Ethel was very old
and I was quite young.
Aunt Elizabeth was a posh,
left-over, thirties antifascist
who asserted her socialism
like a speak-your-weight machine,
but she and my mother's brother
had been comrades since Spain.
Communism united unlikely couples
and they often stayed united.

Elizabeth leads me
and my mum
up lots of creaky stairs
Ethel could never manage
into odoriferous darkness,
evocative of genteel decay.
Elizabeth says Ethel
is looking frail and
eating into her capital.
It'd be bad taste to mention
her state of mind.

Ethel sits at the tea table.
Elizabeth tells her not to mind us.
Ethel says "I went
over the Tay Bridge
two days before it fell down,
Which will be remember'd for a very long time."
Ethel nibbles some shortcake
and sips her tea.

Then she says "I went
over the Tay Bridge
two days before it fell down.
Which will be remember'd for a very long time."
Ethel tries to hold the tea pot
but Elizabeth pours for her.
Ethel puts her hand
in the tin with the castle
on the lid and takes out
another piece of shortcake.
Then she says "I went
over the Tay Bridge
two days before it fell down.
Which will be remember'd for a very long time."

Would anybody remember
The Tay Bridge Disaster
but for William McGonagall?
His poem has been on TV,
so I know all about Ethel.

Sometimes I feel chuffed
when I set down a new poem
as if it were a job well done.
But so did William McGonagall,
Which will be remember'd for a very long time.

Lynn S Meskill

Lion-gate at Mycenae

Turn

No heads.
The roof is gone.
Only the arch remains

and the lion and the lioness,
licking their wounds
with severed tongues.

Counter-Turn

I think the word *severed* is wrong.
Who severed their tongues?
Archaeologists have shown
when the palace roof caved in
the keystone held the vault
in place. Their tongues simply broke
in the tremor that followed.

Stand

The little desk I wrote it on
was a piece of drift-wood
light as air
weathered wood
blown smooth by a Nantucket wind.
Broken, torn, mutilated, rent.
Tongues of land jutting
into the eastern bay — a slip of the tongue
panting tongues of dogs
            the mother tongue
the silence
of Clytemnestra, of Agamemnon.

Their tongues were severed—
Agamemnon executed in his own hall
a purple tapestry of blood
Clytemnestra guillotined by her furious son
cut off—in the middle of a prayer,
like those Tudor queens whose lips
the audience swore
       still moved
after their heads were gone.

Kathryn Ogden

Boxing Day magic

Missing mums,
pieces
of a jigsaw
not there
round the table
with us,
with the boxes
of jam tarts
of mince pies,
sharing a box of
Black Magic or
All Gold
Magic and Gold mums
missing,
boxes not full
but mums very present,
surrounded by their things
living them
acutely
but they are not here
with us
round the table
opening boxes
of jam tarts
of mince pies
of chocolates.

The jigsaw once whole
is no longer,
pieces went missing
but they are present
at the beautiful table set
with their glasses, their dishes,
their cups, their Community Plate.

Feeling their presence
the pieces are back,
an ultimate tribute,
for a short while
on Boxing Day
as when the jigsaw
was complete.

We loved that Boxing Day
in the weirdest way;
the box wasn't full
the jigsaw had lost
some very precious pieces,
we missed them
though we had fun
each with our thoughts
remembering the joy they brought.

But they are around
somewhere
with us,
not far
their presence oozing
from the box
of jam tarts
of mince pies
of chocolates
bitter-sweet.

Pieces of the jigsaw
missing
not lost.

Andrew Sclater

Such Parties, Such Champagne

Now here we are– the birthdays of my life!
she says, inviting me to step with her into a zone
of photographs, where every kiss has long since flown
the lips of all the friends she holds there. Off-the-bone,
devoid of skin and paper-thin, they haven't grown
but stand confined in snapshots, hoping to be known.
She lifts young faces from the box– grey facades of stone
and heavy doors behind– she shrugs, then each is gently thrown
onto the table top. Can all of this be gone?
She points at suns that set decades ago, as if they shone
once more. No cataracts, those days, nor rain. What's done for her
                                        is overrun
by wishfulness. Still every dog lies stiff. No-one
takes her hand or smiles. The champagne bubbles never burst.
The Nescafé she'll make will never slake her thirst.

Andrew Sclater

Dear Mother

Dear Mother, come softly across your grey veil
and onto the path in the dark where the snail
is crossing obliquely and nightjars sing sweetly
and put down your toilet bag quietly, discreetly
on the rim of the cemetery fountain. Now wash
your hair free of this mud and these worms, and squash
the fat maggot that dines in your ears,
then smile as you used to. We'll have no more tears.

Walt Shulits

Rope-A-Pope

(After Francis Bacon's Innocent X)

No, I'm not a malcontent monk or a condescending cultural critic
who snickers at the Vicar, presumes, impugns that there's nothing
papal about this pontiff... but what if his raging religious rectitude
is really just dastardly deceit, what if this pope IS morally bent,

of Satanic descent, sent to earth young boys to torment or maybe
this bloke's a practical joke, a woke masterstroke to evoke might in
the fight against the Christian right, smite its acolytes, which makes
him a buffoon, an opportune cartoon, a metaphoric goon to lampoon.

He looks so suave bedecked in mauve but that pansy purple is pul-
verized, buried by the bordering black, is it the bile of his barbarity
or bitterness from some baneful betrayal... and now behold that he's
trussed in gold, oh how he cajoled, but despite his bulging billfold

he'll never be paroled, perhaps it was something flimflam, financial
scam in the Vatican, gifting a nun a diaphragm(!), the public pissed
that he refused to desist so he was dismissed, is he an alchemist or
the Vicar of tryst, maybe that's the gist but other theories exist,

some critics insist that you need go no farther than Francis and
his father, the dad was bad to the young lad and the painter stayed
mad but despite harbored hatred he found it harder to go furder
than metaphoric murder, papal patricide preferred.

One theory highfalutin but difficult to be disputin', and not meaning
to impeach Nietzsche, to throw his ideas into the breech, but forget
about wanting to deprecate any unholy apostate reprobate, Bacon
simply got it into his head that God herself was surely dead.

An explanation far less banal – and perhaps some might even term it anal – is that he wanted people to hear him "say" that he had an inherent right to be gay even in a sadomasochistic way despite cultural norms in the UK, anyway... he was the shock cock of the walk.

I don't understand the dismissive mystique, the intolerable twaddle of artistic geeks, pedantic poseurs oh so highbrow expecting us peons to be wowed and kowtow, pretentious pundits trying to be what they ain't – not one of them knows how to paint – so I'm not even sure

why I wasted my time in uneven meter but not-too-bad rhyme trying to understand what's the big deal, the nature of this painting's morbid appeal, when I knew at first sight if I recall, despite the crap from the critics' cabal, I'd never want the damn thing on my wall.

Jocelyn Simms

'...crossing the garden by the pale flowers'

– Virginia Woolf

i.m. Helen Dunmore

Six o'clock strikes. Three crows clatter,
chart an opaque sky. Pinpricks of night rain
have etched mysterious footprints
onto brittle tarmac. Frogs crackle.
Mist hedges watery meadows.
No vibration stirs the leaves. No flies.
The garden swing strangulated by its own rope.

Only off-white flowers remain: ivory trumpets,
creamy elders. Bleached stalks of clematis –
the one we'd thought so hardy – snapped.
The church bell chimes the half-hour.
We are inching towards the angelus,
somnambulant, as if we hadn't yet heard.

Jocelyn Simms

Knowing is Believing

Knows how to test a baguette for freshness –
can weigh fruit and veg on the Supermarket
scale – sometimes remembers to stick on the label,

can park his trolley with panache, sometimes
avoids scrapping ankles and jamming toes.

He and I know the sign for water, painted
white on the brisk tarmac road that leads to the river.

We believe flat stones are best for skimming,
we crouch and spin, then let fly our ammunition.

I know his wavy hairline: crinkly curls
that won't simmer down – his chuckle, even his whine,
even his temper –

most of all the way he squeezes my hand
to say, we are the only two who *really* know.

He believes hugs and kisses travel down the phone line,
cross the sea, skip down the road and enter the house
by the front door.

He believes we can lever the Accrington Pals
out from under the memorial stone in the municipal park,
if we only push hard enough.

He knows the Green Man is everywhere
and nowhere, like love and slices of cake.

Gordon Simms

Practising

Heavy emphasis on the first syllable,
a pause before the second,
the rhythm
faltering.

Next door, through an upstairs window,
a head of auburn hair
nods in concentration,
haltingly.
Her mother will be punctual,
confident
of a good report.

I am raking the lawn
at the bottom of the garden
under the sycamore.
Leaves disengage
disturbed by disjointed scales:
they slap onto the wet grass
with one syllable only.
Why mince words?
They, after all, are not
practising.

Helen Steenhuis †

The Calling

I go to your door
and hear you call my name,
but do not answer,
let my name on your voice call
like windows into the night.

I hear my name from your house,
the way you alone will say it,
as if I were my own myth,
or the night itself
waiting to be invited in.

I hear my name on your lips
and do not answer until
my ears have swallowed each letter
with the silence that follows.
Do not answer for the thrill

of the calling, of you looking
for me, while I know –
blended into the darkness
outside your door –
where I am.

Helen Steenhuis †

Yves

Like a child, excited again, he calls
from the ambulance to say it's his turn
to be at the center. Red lights and sirens
pave the way as he glides through the middle lane,
cars parting, dividing like the waters,
his heart skipping beats to keep up.

In Andalusia, he lost sight of her,
his true love, when she ran to visit the church.
Down below, he joined the first line he saw,
Restrooms, where she found him at last,
took his hand in hers, and cackled back up the hill.

We laugh together unaware that this is our last supper:
he moves in stride as I push him up the path,
then follows at his pace,
observing the landscape in his painterly mind.
She stays eight steps ahead 'to keep him on track'.

I can only see you now as on that day,
standing among the pines, boulders above,
the sky blown into an explosion of cloud
like the watercolor on the wall that stops me as I pass.

Marjorie Sweetko

Close reading

From now on, I'll only look at detail –
scrub grass nurtured by rocks,
wind-skipping scurf of weed
daring the sands to catch it,
fragment of plastic film flown
like a flag from a spindly twig
or this, at water's brim: a pebble menhir
abandoned by some tot and swallowing brine -
what's small enough to bend to.

Working from scraps, I'll decipher
lost symbols, let no gravel
seep from my pan: I am not seeking treasure,
just a handle on the land's demotic script;
which, I admit, will need close study,
written, as it is, in a tight, cursive hand
and with its own punctuation – like those two
kitesurfer commas there, or the parenthesis of Africa
plodding past, crying *bandanas, good prices*.

Marjorie Sweetko

Caged

Here comes morning's torch through my bars,
searching for the usual suspects,
fugitive twigs, wandering bracts
of bougainvillea, whatever elects
freedom and might give me ideas,

though flight's increasingly hard to construe,
when every autumn hammers in a rail of gold,
when each spring adds a shiny bolt
and I shuffle closer to the shadows, to you.

I'm tamed, complicit, accomplished at arranging
traces, draping memory and mime
harmoniously. There's a trick to managing
solitary, I've heard, and that's to become
convinced the cage is actually home.

In a while, I'll check the climber's tendrils are secure,
inspect for white fly or withered leaf
and plump the cushions, simple ways to leave
my imprint, a scent, some signature.

Tom Vaughan

Swot

It's time to hunker down and swot
with coffee as my only friend

and each dawn closer to the end
which in the distance I can spot:

the happiness which lies ahead
when I'll have passed with flying colours

and on a day unlike all others
will saunter through the streets instead.

I won't be bored, I tell myself:
the world will sparkle, and the hours

will sprinkle down in golden showers.
I won't need anything – my wealth

will be the knowledge I'll forget
and which I haven't learnt as yet.

Tom Vaughan

Happiness

It's easy to forget they'd fought a war:
his father drowned, half-brother bayoneted;
her kilted sibling captured at Dunkirk,
locked up for five long years. But yes they met

in uniform, lost half their friends, before
the normal world re-started when they wed:
mortgage; children; grinding office work –
all I suppose they wanted when they set

out as a couple. We must have been a shock:
busting their rulebook; scornful of sacrifice;
mocking their past and their belief in 'progress';

too young, too smashed, too angry to unlock
their silence, or to understand the price
they'd paid for what they'd still call happiness.

Mehran Waheed

Cheddar Man

Some day I will go to Aarhus
To see his peat-brown head...
        — Seamus Heaney, *The Tollund Man*

I

Year after year, I have passed your deathplace,
Driving through Somerset's skull.
Searching to carve surf,
Cut waves of teeth, on the
West country's coast.

Ignorant, to chiselled veins beneath
River Axe and Cheddar Yeo.
Their sump of memory,
Our nation's thready pulse
Coming up for air.

II

They scalpelled a trench, dug inside
Mother England's turf
Of verdant curls.
Scraped her deep, dank
Fallopian caves.

She clutched, then recoiled her
Stalagmite fingers, when they
Snatched you away, suckling under
The crevice, hidden against her
Limestone breasts.

Fossilised, but like a foetus
They celebrated the harvest,
Piled a cairn of your bones,
Weighed time from drilled petrous,
Tagged you wrist to toe.

III

One tenth prodigal father,
Younger than me, your adopted son,
You are their monstrous creator,
Blacker than they
Tried to conceive.

I could claim chromatocracy,
My Maghreb skin now
Closer to pride's dark history.
Muddied flesh they would deny,
Bred apart from your blood.

Eyes dipped in the North Sea,
Doggerland treachery,
Tanned wax mocks them,
Patriotism's paucity —
Only you would know for sure,

Your flag's true borne colours.

Chris Welch

Cigarettes and rain

When I heard that you had gone from here,
I wondered what had made you move so fast,
leaving friends and lovers to enquire
which of us had killed time with you last.

The coffee bar is busy, but quiet at the back.
Your usual table waits – it doesn't know you've gone.
I'm out of fags – can't steal one from your pack.
Can't work out why and what it is I've done.

The rainy streets are trite but fit my mood.
I shamble greyly past our one-time haunts,
wondering at my feeling so subdued
and why it's now my heart knows what it wants.

I read the message your departure sends.
This is where it starts, or this is how it ends.

Alice White

Answering Her Question

My sister taught me a parenting trick
for when kids ask a difficult question
like 'Is Santa Claus real?' or 'What is sex?'
Simply ask, in earnest, 'What do *you* think?'
and listen. At the least, it buys you time.
My daughter, three, in the car one evening,
is silent. Then asks, 'Mama, will *I* die?'
I just drive. Try to keep the car tethered
to the earth. Somehow the trick surfaces
within me and I ask, 'What do *you* think?'
In the rearview mirror I see her smile
looking out at the purple sky. She says
'I think I will *never* die.' I tell her
'That's what I think, too.' And I do, I do.

Alice White

Girl in the Woods

I get glimpses of her in pictures, in
a t-shirt and no underwear, before
she cared, or bareback on a horse before
the branch. Before boobs, before boys. Before
school she was everywhere, that much is sure –
before the world condensed into a shape
to fit into. Some days I can sense her:
I disappeared from a girl scout campout
to commandeer a wooden raft I found,
looking. My counsellor shook her head, just said
I wouldn't have expected this of you.
Whenever I think I've got hold of her,
she kicks my shin and wriggles from my grasp,
runs for the trees, calls back, *Try and catch me –*

Patrick Williamson

Crossings

The swell of lift & descent
in the dark a howling wet wind
here we go, half way up, then
pitch again, toss & plunge,
hold on, for life is not drowning.

Softly, like a whisper, the surf
releases, o my god,
its tongue reaches, eyes wide open,
its next breath draws in
harsh & rasping, the rush of silence
the sated wind sweeps up, love
clutching fingers break free
sliding back, tugged by undertow.

I was a child too, imagined
shadowy creatures reach up
& strip away the covers –
the cold, we are joined
myself, black-blue sea,
swept away, swirling rafts
skating over the fathoms.

Patrick Williamson

The trace we leave behind

The word on the page is unscarred
and writing the glue,
only replicants seal wounds cleanly
so no trace remains;
we always leave a trace,
an identity in the cloud, portrait with Gray,
perfect to leave our ugliness behind.

These quarrels of ourselves, this life
we're bound upon is messy;
predators or stars, we rise and fall
the right road lost and gone,
and when the dark wood surrounds us
we leave scarred tissues behind,
so make our life a poem, on the page.

Contributors

Sharon Black is from Glasgow and lives in a remote valley of the Cévennes mountains. She won *The London Magazine* Poetry Prizes 2019 and 2018. She has published four full collections of poetry and a pamphlet. Her latest collections are *The Last Woman Born on the Island* (Vagabond Voices), exploring Scotland's culture and heritage, and *The Red House* (Drunk Muse), set in France. She is editor of Pindrop Press. *www.sharonblack.co.uk*

Nina Bogin (USA/France), poet and translator, recipient of an NEA grant for poetry, lives in northeastern France. Her poetry collections are *In the North* (Graywolf); *The Winter Orchards* and *The Lost Hare* (Anvil); and *Thousandfold* (Carcanet); as well as *The Illiterate* by Agota Kristof (translation of *L'analphabète*) published by CB Editions and New Directions. Her poems have appeared in magazines and anthologies in the USA, UK, Canada and France.

Beverley Bie Brahic is a Canadian poet and translator who has published five collections. *White Sheets* (CB Editions) was a 2013 Forward Prize finalist and also a PBS Recommendation as was *The Hunting of the Boar* (CB Editions), three years later. Her Apollinaire translation, *The Little Auto*, won the Scott Moncrieff Translation Prize. Her latest collection, *Apple Thieves*, is published by Carcanet in 2024. She lives in Paris.

Nejra Ćehić is a British-Bosnian poet born to Bosnian and Chinese Malaysian parents, growing up in Kuala Lumpur, Sarajevo and Cardiff, Wales. Her poetry appears in *Poetry Wales, Ink Sweat & Tears, 14 magazine* and elsewhere. She was longlisted for the Queen Mary Wasafiri New Writing Prize (Poetry). She currently lives in Voiron and is working on her first full-length collection.

For **Jennefer Cole**, an East Coast American, poetry allows her to voice various identities as a woman, wife, mother and daughter. After studying linguistics and literature at university, she came to

France to teach for one year. Thirty years later, she is still learning, teaching, and enjoying the expat experience. She has published poetry in *The Broadkill Review*, *FLAR*, and *erbacce press* and prose in *Atlande Press* and *The English Media Centre*.

David Crann, an English solicitor, became a wholesaler of English books in Provence before retiring. His interests include family, travel, poetry, music, bridge, gardening. Published in *Orbis*, *The French Literary Review*, *Dream Catcher*, *Earlyworks*, *Poetry Salzburg*. *Barnet Poetry*, *Littoral Press Poetry*, *Cerasus Poetry*, *The Piker Press*, he has also been selected in numerous competitions: Earlyworks (first), Barnet Borough Council (first), Speakeasy, Mary Charman-Smith, Teignmouth, Sentinel, Welsh Poetry, Long Poem Magazine.

Anne Eyries left the UK last century to work in France. Her writing has appeared or is forthcoming in *Dream Catcher*, *The Piker Press*, *The Hyacinth Review*, *Mslexia* and *Reflex Press*, amongst others.

Gill Foster, originally from Scarborough, Yorkshire, is a retired college lecturer. She has written poetry and has published short stories for many years. Most of her poems are in narrative form, telling tales which are at times wryly humorous and at times sombre. Aged eighty, and after twenty-two years in France, her urge to write has not wavered with the passing of time. She lives in Roquefort, in the Landes region.

Mary Gilonne is a translator living near Aix-en-Provence, but hails from Devon. She has won the Wenlock, Segora, Wirral, Sentinel, Poetry on the Lake and Pen Nib prizes, and been shortlisted for the Bridport. Placed in The Plough, Yaffle, Bedford, Prole, Spelt competitions among others, her work has been published in *Magma*, *Antiphon*, *Strix* ..., and anthologies. Her pamphlet *Incidentals* is published by 4Word Press and her collection *Sublimity* by Sublime Norfolk Publishing.

Born and raised in Scotland, **Kathleen Gray** left home at eighteen for London, The Hague and Paris, which became home. She studied creative writing at Oxford University. Her poems and short fiction have appeared in *Pharos, Reflex fiction, New Feathers Anthology, Piker Press, Drawn by the Light* and *Dreich*.

Nicholas Henshall was born in Manchester and grew up in northern England. He now lives in Paris where he works as a journalist. Nicholas loves long conversations, new destinations and poetry. His work has been published in the *Buddhist Poetry Review*, Buddhist arts magazine *Urthona*, and *www.yourdailypoem.com*. His favourite literary lines are the soliloquy, 'What light is light if Silvia be not seen?' from *The Two Gentlemen of Verona*.

Kate Hill-Charalambides was born and educated in London. She has lived in France for more than forty years and has dual nationality. Kate studied and taught English at University Jean-Jaures in Toulouse. She has been actively involved in an association recognised as being of public utility which helps the victims of human trafficking to obtain asylum. Her chosen poem, published in *Dreich*, was triggered by her voluntary work.

Jill Husser has lived and worked in Strasbourg for more than thirty years. Her work has been published in *Poetry Scotland, Dreich* and the *Amethyst Review*.

Christopher M James, a dual British/French national and retired HR professional, has published in *Acumen, Aesthetica, Magma, Orbis, Dream Catcher, London Grip, Poetry Salzburg, IS & T, The London Magazine, Best New British and Irish poetry 2019-2021*, amongst others. He has been a prize winner in a number of competitions (Sentinel, Hastings, Yeovil, Stroud, Poets meet Politics, Wirral, Buzzwords, Torbay...) and has been widely anthologised. He lives in the Dordogne.

Shirin Jindani holds a PhD on Irish poetry and textiles. Her publications include the book chapter 'Intertextuality and Autology' (Finding a language) and a peer-reviewed article 'For 'text' read 'textile': Paul Muldoon's poetic weaving'. She was shortlisted for the Bridport Poetry Prize and Highly Commended in the Westport Poetry Competition. Her poetry has appeared in the anthology *Poems from Pandemia*, as well as in the journals *Envoi* and *Staple*.

Charlie Lomas was born in Manchester. He has history degrees from Leeds and London universities. Playful humour in his writing reflects an ironic attitude to human beings; our unperceptiveness, our cruelty and our appropriation of the earth. He has lived in a Cévennes village for thirty-one years, working as a translator.

Lynn S Meskill is Professor of Early Modern English Literature at the University of Toulouse. She is author of *Ben Jonson and Envy* (Cambridge University Press), a translation and edition of a seventeenth-century French treatise by Marguerite Buffet, *New Observations on the French Language, with Praises of Illustrious Learned Women* (Iter Press), and articles on Jonson, Shakespeare and Milton. Four of her poems appeared in *Seneca Review*.

Kathryn Ogden's foray into poetry began during a particularly difficult period of her life, when she found the poetic form the natural way to express that vulnerability she was feeling at the time. Some of her deeply personal poems have never been shared. Others have been shared mostly with the extended family. Kathryn lives near Paris and works internationally as a nutritionist in the humanitarian and development sector.

Andrew Sclater lives in Paris, spending spells in Scotland and Norway. Recipient of awards from New Writing North and the Scottish Book Trust, he was shortlisted for the Picador Poetry Prize. *Dinner at the Blaws-Baxters'* was published by HappenStance. A new selection is forthcoming from Mariscat in 2025.

Walt Shulits is a retired bond market professional and lifelong paddling fanatic – sea kayak, outrigger canoe and surf ski – who stumbled upon poetry while searching for an activity giving him the same sense of living in the moment. Residing in Provence, he spends as much time as possible in Hawaii. He writes poems for the multitudes who find poetry as incomprehensible as Sanskrit, as unappealing as mountain oysters.

Jocelyn Simms has lived in France since 2002 where she has organised three bilingual literary festivals and Segora international writing competitions 2007-2022. Publications: *Colour Matters*, stimuli for creative writing, *Tickling the Dragon*, birth of the nuclear age (Circaidy Gregory), winner of the Poetry Book of the Year Award, 2020. *Grisailles*, poems and photographs of her locality (Hey Editions), *The Promise of Thaw*, poetry collection (erbacce press).

Gordon Simms enjoyed a career in the performing arts. *Judas*, an anthology of dance, poetry and music was broadcast in 1968 (BBC TV). Publications: *Introducing Seed Collage* (Batsford); a double bill, *Stop Press* and *Time Out* (New Theatre Publications); *Uphill to the Sea*, poetry collection (Biscuit Press); a novella, *Open Strings* (Cinnamon), currently being translated into French. Collaborated with Jocelyn Simms on festivals, workshops and Segora.

Originally from Atlanta, **Helen Steenhuis** lived near Aix-en-Provence. She taught the English language, brought a sunny simplicity to her daily activities, wrote little but well, often in the elegiac mode, and admired Emily Dickinson, James Dickey and Edgar Bowers in particular. Helen died in January 2024. Her poems have appeared in *The French Literary Review, Equinox: A Poetry Journal, The Poetry Library, Southbank London, Cumberland River Review*, and *Amethyst Review*.

Marjorie Sweetko's poetry has been widely published in journals including *The North, Magma, Poetry Salzburg Review, Artemis Poetry, South, The London Magazine* and in the Poetry Business anthology *One for the Road*. Born in Canada, she lived in London and Sussex, then in Morocco, Thailand and Italy, before settling in the 1990s in Marseilles.

Former British diplomat **Tom Vaughan**'s previous publications include a novel and three poetry collections, the latest entitled *Just a Minute* (Cyberwit, 2024). His poems have appeared in a range of poetry and current affairs magazines, and in anthologies. *Beltway Blues* from the *Envoy* collection was included in the Songs of Love and Loss cycle by pianist/composer Sir Stephen Hough, premiered in a Wigmore Hall concert in 2023.

Mehran Waheed is a winner of the Wasafiri New Writing Poetry Prize. His work has been published by *Live Canon*, *Hedgehog* and *Tindal Street Press*. He was shortlisted for the Robert Graves Prize. Mehran currently lives in Toulouse.

Chris Welch is a former academic turned consultant based in Strasbourg since 2011. He writes very slowly and has never previously had anything published. His most significant poetry-related achievement to date was to author a site-specific pantoum, which spent four years on the International Space Station between 2019 and 2023.

Alice White is an American poet who lives in Arnac-Pompadour, Corrèze. A 2022 Hawthornden Fellow, she was shortlisted for the 2023 Aesthetica and Magma prizes and selected for *Best New Poets*. Her poetry has recently appeared in *The Poetry Review, berlin lit, The Dark Horse, The London Magazine, Mslexia, Poetry Scotland*, and *The Threepenny Review*, and has been featured on the podcast *The Slowdown*. She can be found at ***www.poetalicewhite.com***

Patrick Williamson lives near Paris and is an English poet and translator. Latest poetry collection: *Presence/Presenza* (Samuele Editore, 2023). Editor and translator of *Turn your back on the night, ten poets from Africa and the Arab World* (The Antonym), and translator notably of Tahar Bekri and Erri de Luca. Active in projects with artists' book publisher Transignum in France. Member of the European board of The Antonym.

Acknowledgements

The publisher gratefully acknowledges the poets' permission to reproduce their work from the following magazines, books and sources:

Sharon Black: 'Café des Arts' in *Poetry Ireland Review;* 'Folio' in *The Friday Poem.*
Nina Bogin: 'The Swifts' in *Hudson Review;* 'Wooden Spoons in *At Home Anthology* (Lautus Press).
Beverley Bie Brahic: 'Tango' in *Apple Thieves* (Carcanet); 'The Origin of Art' in *Hunting the Boar* (CB Editions).
Nejra Ćehić: 'I read some poets' in *Poetry Wales;* 'a request' in *Smoke Magazine.*
David Crann: 'When I am an old man' in *Cote Poets.*
Anne Eyries: 'The End of Endurance 1915' in *The Hyacinth Review.*
Mary Gilonne: 'Papermaker' in *52 Anthology;* 'It will happen by chance' in *Whirlagust 1V,* reprinted in *Sublimity* (Sublimity Norfolk Press).
Kathleen Gray: 'Déjà Vu' in *New Feathers Anthology.*
Kate Hill-Charalambides: 'Burnt Milk' in *Dreich.*
Jill Husser: 'Birthing' in *Poetry Scotland.*
Christopher M James: 'Marshes' in *Stanza Competition, Poetry Society;* 'Traces' in *Acumen,* reprinted in *Aesthetica.*
Shirin Jindani: '#MakingFriends' in *Poems from Pandemia* (Southwood).
Lynn S Meskill: 'Lion-gate at Mycenae' in *Seneca Review.*
Andrew Sclater: 'Such Parties, Such Champagne' in *Ambit,* and 'Dear Mother' in *Poetry Review.*
Jocelyn Simms: '...crossing the garden by the pale flowers' and 'Knowing is Believing' in *The Promise of Thaw* (erbacce).
Gordon Simms: 'Practising' in *Uphill to the Sea* (Biscuit Press).
Marjorie Sweetko: 'Close reading' in *Antiphon;* 'Caged' in *Poetry Salzburg.*
Tom Vaughan: 'Swot' in *Snakeskin;* 'Happiness' in *Dream Catcher.*
Alice White: 'Answering Her Question' in *New Letters;* 'Girl in the Woods' in *The Poetry Review.*
Patrick Williamson: 'Crossings' in *Traversi;* 'The trace we leave behind' in *Traversi,* reprinted in *Noon.*

www.ingramcontent.com/pod-product-compliance
Lightning Source LLC
Chambersburg PA
CBHW011800040426

42447CB00015B/3455